YOUR KNOWLEDGE HAS VALUE

Magdalena Zettl

Coordinating National Poverty Reduction Strategy Papers and the Millennium Development Goals

A Case Study on the 'Absorption' of MDG 2 and MDG 5 in Ethiopia's Poverty Reduction and Growth Strategies

GRIN Verlag

Bibliografische Information der Deutschen Nationalbibliothek:

Die Deutsche Bibliothek verzeichnet diese Publikation in der Deutschen National-
bibliografie; detaillierte bibliografische Daten sind im Internet über http://dnb.d-
nb.de/ abrufbar.

Imprint:

Copyright © 2012 GRIN Verlag GmbH
Druck und Bindung: Books on Demand GmbH, Norderstedt Germany
ISBN: 978-3-656-57111-7

This book at GRIN:

http://www.grin.com/en/e-book/266410/coordinating-national-poverty-reduction-
strategy-papers-and-the-millennium

Coordinating National Poverty Reduction Strategy Papers and the Millennium Development Goals - A Case Study on the 'Absorption' of MDG 2 and MDG 5 in Ethiopia's Poverty Reduction and Growth Strategies

Final Term Paper
Poverty, Inequality and Growth, 2013
Magdalena Zettl

Abstract

Poverty reduction strategy papers (PRSPs) are claimed to be the 'crucial link' between the Millennium Development Goals (MDGs) on the global level and poverty reduction and growth strategies on the nation level as PRSPs incorporate more and more MDG goals and indicators. Ethiopia, a low-income country in Sub-Saharan Africa, is used as a case study as it has not only made significant advancements in terms of achieving the MDG goals since 2000 but has also made extensive use of PRSPs. Ethiopia has already issued its third generation of PRSPs (2002; 2006; 20011), including an interim PRSP in 2000. The essay analyzes how well MDG 2 'Primary Universal Education' and MDG 5 'Maternal Health' have been absorbed into Ethiopia's PRSPs. Findings confirm that PRSPs are a crucial means to implement MDGs within national policies and programs. Moreover, the study hints to how different processes of MDG incorporation into PRSPs influence the achievement of the respective MDGs on the national level. PRSPs have to be given considerable importance in the post-2015 agenda; however, a revision of PRSPs is urgently needed to compensate PRSP's criticism and its lack in adhering to some of its most crucial principles, which play a significant role in the post 2015-agenda.

Table of Content

1 Introduction

Poverty Reduction Strategy Papers (PRSPs) are an initiative, launched in 1999 in a joint effort of the World Bank and the International Monetary Fund (IMF), to encourage poverty reduction in low-income countries (LIC) through appropriate national policies: LICs are supposed to create "macro-economic, structural and social policies" to ensure growth and reduction of poverty; in turn, the IMF and the World Bank provide access to concessional loans, debt relief and multilateral development assistance (World Bank, 2013a). Since then, PRSPs have become a widely used policy tool by LICs: until today, 67 countries have prepared PRSPs, 37 issued the second generation of PRSPs and 5 have already published their third PRSP (World Bank, 2012). Nevertheless, several scholars criticize the effectiveness of PRSPs. Among the most important negative points are the missing link between PRSPs and the long-term problem of inequality; a lack of institutions and governments to implement PRSPs; the contradiction of ownership of the PRSPs on the one hand but conditionality imposed by the IMF and the World Bank on the other hand (Adejumobi, 2006; Oxfam, 2004; Fraser, 2005).

Despite this critique, PRSPs are regarded as the main tool for achieving the global agenda of poverty reduction, the Millennium Development Goals (MDGs), on the national level. Both, MDGs and PRSPs, aim at poverty reduction through clearly defined targets and put a strong focus on country ownership. Moreover, both are led by the same organizations, i.e. the World Bank and the IMF (Eggen, 2008: 1-4). According to Eggen (2008), the MDGs present a set of internationally agreed development priorities, while PRSPs are an "approach to formulating [development] policies" on the national level (2). The IMF makes the relation between MDGs and PRSPs even clearer by describing the PRSPs as "the crucial link (...) to meet the MDGs" (IMF, 2013a). Scholars, such as Kalinda (2008), consider PRSPs as "the country-level operational framework for progress towards the (...) MDGs" (1). According to research of Bucki et al. (2013), Hulme & Fukudu-Parr (2009) and Picard (2010), the MDGs are gradually incorporated into PRSPs, however, to a different extent depending on the country context.

Using Ethiopia as a case study, the essays provides a comparative analysis on the absorption of the MDGs in Ethiopia's PRSPs by focusing on MDG 2 'Primary Universal Education' and MDG 5 'Maternal Health'. Firstly, the essay provides relevant background information on PRSPs in general, on the development context of Ethiopia as well as on the relation between MDGs and PRSPs in Ethiopia. In its main part, the paper analyzes how MDG 2 and MDG 5 have been incorporated into Ethiopia's PRSPs by focusing on the adoption of the respective MDG targets and indicators in PRSPs since 2000. The study shows that both MDGs have been successfully included in Ethiopia's PRSPs; however, their process of absorption was different. Trying to provide an explanation for this, the essay refers back to the comprehensive-principle of PRSPs as national governments, domestic and external development partners have distinct priorities. The impact of these different processes of absorption is visible in the current status of achieving MDG 2 and MDG 5. Based on the analysis, the essay concludes by giving an outlook on PRSP's role in the post-2015 agenda: as national poverty reduction and growth strategies they might hinder to successfully absorb and tackle crosscutting poverty issues which, in turn, challenges PRSP's future role in the post-2015 agenda of Sustainable Development Goals (SDG).

2 Context

2.1 Poverty Reduction Strategy Papers

As aforementioned, PRSPs are a controversial but highly used policy tool by LICs to receive concessional loans and aid from multilateral donors, i.e. the IMF and the World Bank. PRSPs underlie the following set of principles: country-ownership, result-oriented, comprehensive, partnership-oriented, long-term perspective. Hence, through PRSPs, countries take responsibility for their own problems and development by defining clear means of measurement to track the results. Moreover, PRSPs are supposed to tackle all dimension of poverty and are compiled in cooperation with all stakeholders, i.e. domestic groups, government, donors, development partners, and are designed for three years or more. PRSPs usually consist of an analysis of the country's current poverty situation, a description of national policies and programs aimed to execute to reduce poverty and an overview of financial needs and funding sources (IMF, 2013a; 2013b).

2.2 Development background: Ethiopia

Ethiopia, a developing, low-income country in the Sub-Saharan region has the second highest population in Africa and is economically highly dependent on the service sector and agriculture, with coffee being its main product of export (CIA Factsheet, 2013). Recurring droughts and consequences of climate change are highly impacting the population as well as poverty rates. According to World Bank (2013a) data of 2011, 30.7% live in extreme poverty and the Gini Index is 33.6. However, rural poverty, which is at 80%, is the government's main challenge.

In terms of the MDGs, Africa is largely lacking behind in reaching the MDGs, however the continent has made major advancements since 2000, especially due to economic growth (UNDP, 2013: 6). Ethiopia has played a key role in this regard, as it is among the top performing countries in Sub-Saharan Africa with the best improvements for target 1B, Indicator 3.2 and target 7C (Provost, 2013; UNDP, 2013). Also, the 2010 MDG Report and MDG Track (2010) show that Ethiopia is doing better than the rest of its region: it has already or will achieve the majority of MDG indicators of MDG1, 2, 6 and 8 by 2015 or latest 2020. At the same time, as of 2010, Ethiopia is struggling with the rest of the MDGs, especially with crosscutting poverty issues such as gender equality, infant mortality, maternal health and environmental sustainability (achievement forecasted after 2025). However, the MDG Report 2013 on Africa as well as the MDG Progress Index (Provost, 2013) indicate that Ethiopia's progress on these MDGs has highly advanced and, contrary to observations of 2010, some of these might be achieved by 2015.

In terms of PRSPs, the African region has by far been most active in issuing and adhering to PRSPs: 34 of 67 PRSPs are from the African region (World Bank, 2012). With Ethiopia having published its third generation of PRPs in 2011, this country makes an interesting case study as it combines major achievements in MDGs with great efforts in terms of PRSPs. Also, the changes in forecast from 2010 to 2013 might be explained by a closer look at the most recent PRSP (2010/11-2014/5).

2.3 MDGs and PRSPs in Ethiopia

Since the 1990s Ethiopia was concerned with poverty reduction, economic growth and human development. Its main tool to tackle these was through Structural Adjustment Programs (SAPs). However, when the IMF/World Bank launched PRSPs, Ethiopia immediately issued an interim PRPS in 2000 which was ousted by the first full PRSP, called 'Sustainable Development and Poverty Reduction Program' (SDPRP), in 2002. Here, Ethiopia's main focus was on an economic growth of 7% in order to reduce poverty. In 2005, a second PRSP was published, the Plan for Accelerated and Sustained Development to End Poverty (PASDEP), laying out a clear poverty reduction strategy until 2010. The third generation of Ethiopia's PRSP focused on another 5-year-period and was issued in 2011: the Poverty Reduction Strategy Paper Growth and Transformation Plan (GTP) 2010/11-2014/15 (IMF, 2013b; Afrodad, 2006: 7-9; MoFED, 2010: 1-2; Ministry of Foreign Affairs, 2013).

The MDGs were officially incorporated into Ethiopia's development policies after the 2005 MDG Needs Assessment by the Ethiopian government and other development stakeholders (MoFED, 2006: 2; MoFED, 2000; MoFED, 2002). Nevertheless, the SDPRP already focused on reduction of poverty and hunger, primary education as well as reducing HIV/Aids transmission; it used several MDG indicators to track progress and, thereby, already showed strong relations to the MDGs (Afrodad, 2010: 13-14; MoFED, 2002). The second generation of Ethiopian PRSP, the PASDEP, emphasized to continue with the priorities set out in the SDPRP and added a focus on growth of the private sector and agriculture. Most importantly, the PASDEP entails "scaling up efforts to achieve the Millennium Development Goals" and is, thereby, "harmonizing (...) [Ethiopian's] PRSP and the MDGs" (Afrodad, 2010: 14): for the first time, targets of Ethiopia's PRSP are directly and clearly linked with the relevant MDG goal and the respective MDG indicators (or similar indicators established) (MoFED, 2006: 248-250). Nevertheless, several weaknesses in fully incorporating the MDGs in Ethiopia's PRSPs become already apparent in these early stages: so-called 'cross-cutting issues' are not properly represented in the PASDEP, especially gender equality, environment and global partnerships for development (Afrodad, 2010: 16; MoFED, 2006). The most current PRSP, the GTP, which outlines Ethiopia's poverty reduction strategy until 2015, the same year as the end of the MDGs, puts increased emphasis not only on economic growth (through increased productivity in the agricultural and industry sector) but also on social development (through improving education and health services, especially maternal mortality). In an extremely clearly and detailed way, the GTP relates its defined strategy to the MDGs, outlining exactly which GTP goal refers to which MDG including the usage of MDG indicators and annual targets. GTP's targets are mostly consistent with MDG targets (MoFED, 2011; World Bank, 2013b; Ministry of Foreign Affairs, 2013).

3 'Absorption' of MDGs in Ethiopia's PRSPs (2000-2015)

3.1 Case study I: MDG 2 and educational policies in Ethiopia

MDG 2, "achieving universal primary education", is measured by three indicators: ratio of net primary education enrolment (2.1); completion of primary schools for students starting in grade 1 (2.2); literacy rate (2.3) (UNDP, 2008).

Primary education has long been a central issue of Ethiopia's poverty reduction and growth strategy: based on the Education and Training Policy (ETP) of 1994, the 'five-year Education Sector Development Programme' (ESDP) was established in 1995, aiming to increase enrollment into primary schools from 22.1% in 1995/6 to 60% by 2001/2. The I-PRSP adopted this goal and set a respective target for Gross Enrollment Ratio (primary) (GERP). Moreover, the I-PRSP established goals for increasing the number and quality of as well as access to primary schools. At the same time, education of teachers was to improve through further education programs and rural schooling should be strengthened through mobile education programs (MoDEF, 2000: 10-14). The I-PRSP already made clear reference to the MDG by comparing its own targets and indicators to the 'International Development Goals', however, except the common indicator of GERP, the I-PRSP did not overlap with the International Development Goals. In fact, the I-PRSP went far beyond the actual MDG 2 (MoDEF, 2000: 25). Literacy rate and the percentage of students finishing primary school were hardly mentioned in the I-PRSP.

The SDPRP was accompanied by the second phase of the aforementioned ESDP. The main target for primary education was to raise the GERP to 65% by 2004/5. Thereby, the SDPRP made clear reference to MDG Indicator 2.1. Additional to that, the SDPRP focused on quality of schools and teachers and the improvement of syllabi and textbooks. Aside from similar goals set for secondary, tertiary, adult, special needs and vocational education, primary education was, by far, allocated the most money: 46.1% of total budget on development policies (MoDEF, 2002: 89-97). However, similar to the I-PRSP, there was no information on the other MDG Indicators 2.2 and 2.3 (MoDEF, 2002: 157; UN, 2008). The SDPRP provided an analysis of literacy in Ethiopia and "national-level adult literacy programs" were to be built (172). However, there was no reference to the respective MDG and also no mentioning of a specific target for literacy rate.

The PASDEP was a true advancement in incorporating MDG 2 into Ethiopia's PRSP for 2005/6 - 2009/10: besides setting a further target for GERP (about 86.6%), the PASDEP also included primary education completion rates as a target, thus, referring to MDG indicator 2.1 and 2.3. Moreover, the PASPED aimed to establish more in-depth programs to address the defined indicators, for example an alternative basic education program for pastoral and rural areas, redesigned teaching strategies for older children and multi-grade classroom teaching (MoFED, 2006: 111-112). National policies and programs working towards primary education and supporting these targets were the continuation of the ESDP and the 'National Plan of Action for Ethiopian Children (2004-2010)'. In terms of spending, primary education was again "top priority" (MoFED, 2006: 210). As of of literacy, the PASDEP mentioned how literacy improved since 1995/6 and more programs fighting literacy were to be initiated, however, again, there was no clear literacy target defined.

The currently running GTP is strongly linked to MDG 2 and gives exact indicators and targets for primary education: these do not only include the official MDG 2 indicators but go well beyond those. Moreover, targets such as 100% school enrolment for girls and boys are consistent with MDG 2 (MoFED, 2011: 19-20).

The analysis shows that primary education, specifically primary school enrollment, has long been part of Ethiopia's poverty reduction and growth strategy. Actions towards achieving the GERP have manifested themselves over a time span of more than 20 years and could fully develop their potential. Thus, the link between MDG 2 and the PRSP was already well established before 2000. Nevertheless, the full scope of MDG 2 has been incorporated extremely well over the years and Ethiopia's PRSPs have more and more adapted to this MDG: primary school completion rates, which were not part of the SDRPR, were included in the PASDEP. The literacy rate was mentioned in the SDRPP only, however, received increased attention in the PASDEP and was fully absorbed in the GTP. The fact that primary school enrollment and primary school completion rates have been part of Ethiopia's politics since 2005 have highly contributed to the fact that Ethiopia is on track achieving these indicators by 2015 while the late incorporation of the literacy rate, among other reasons, can be accountable why the achievement of this indicator by 2015 is being questioned (Provost, 2013).

3.2 Case study II: MDG 5 and health policies in Ethiopia

MDG 5 consists of two targets: reducing the maternal mortality rate by 75% until 2015 (5A); universal access to reproductive health (5B). These goals are measured by the following six indicators: maternal mortality ratio (5.1) and rate of births attended by trained personnel (5.2), which refer to goal 5A; contraceptive prevalence rate (5.3), adolescent birth rate (5.4), pre-natal care coverage (5.5) and unmet need for family planning (5.6), referring to goal 5B (UNDP, 2008).

Similar to the GERP, decreasing the maternal mortality rate (MMR) was an integral part of Ethiopia's poverty reduction and growth strategy since the beginning. In the I-PRSP, MMR was supposed to be reduced from 705/100 000 to 500/100 000 and a clear link to the International Development Goal was established. However, the MMR is the only measure the I-PRSP refers to, which coincides with an indicator of today's MDG 5, namely indicator 5.1. The I-PRSP does not mention any of the other MDG indicators for goal 5. Neither does the I-PRSP refer to exact details how a reduction of the MMR should be achieved. It only refers to the multi-year Health Sector Development Program (HSDP

I) aiming at improving the quantity and quality of doctors, primary health care services and hospitals with an increased budget for the health sector (MoFED, 2000).

In the SDPRP, maternal health is defined as one of the "priority areas" (MoDEF, 2002: 150): MMR is aimed to decrease further from 500-700 to 400-500 of 100 000 by 2005 and to 300 by 2017. This shows that achieving the MDG 5 on MMR, i.e. reduction of MMR by three quarters, will be extremely difficult for Ethiopia. Nevertheless, this target was ambitiously set and further incorporated in Ethiopia's PRSPs. Additionally, the first actual PRSP included the reduction of fertility rate to 4% by 2015, increase of contraceptive prevalence rate to 44% by 2015 and increase in attendance of births by trained health personnel from 16% in 2002 to 25% in 2005, thereby using MDG indicators 5.1, 5.2, 5.3 and 5.4 (MoDEF, 2002: 122). However, the SDPRP still misses out on including MDG indicators 5.5, and 5.6 referring only vaguely to family planning and to pre-natal check-ups not at all. In terms of policies, Ethiopia implemented the HSDP II including a Health Extension Package aiming to improve access to and awareness for health as well as health prevention (MoDEF, 2002: 44; 97-100). The SDPRP ensures "a consideration of the Millennium Development Goals" in the HSDP II (100). Strategies outlined to achieve the aforementioned goals were clear and appeared well thought through. Hence, compared to the I-PRPS, the SDPRP presented a real advancement in terms of absorbing MDG 5, even before the MDG Needs Assessment with the Ethiopian government.

In the PASDEP, aforementioned targets were adjusted, e.g. MMR, which was at 871/100 000 in 2005, was aimed to be reduced to 600 by 2010; coverage of contraceptive prevalence was to be further increased to 60% and target of fertility rate of 4% for 2010 kept. Services on family planning were said to be introduced; wording used in the PASDEP was very similar to the MDGs, for example "addressing the unmet demand of family planning" (MoDEF, 2006: 50). Additionally, antenatal care was explicitly mentioned for the first time in the PASDEP. The national policy and program plan HSDP III worked alongside this PRSP by giving priority to maternal health and focusing on preventive health care services.

In the current GTP, defined goals for maternal health and indicators are almost the same as for the official MDG 5. Targets are mostly consistent with the official MDG 5 goals, however, some had to be reduced as initial levels were too far away from the actual target. This shows that MDG 5 has been fully absorbed into Ethiopia's PRSP.

The analysis shows that MMR was adopted already in Ethiopia's I-PRSP and received increasing importance over the years. Most adaptions in terms of MDG 5 were already made in the second generation of Ethiopia's PRSP by adding fertility rate, prevalence rate, pre-natal care and the mentioning of family planning into the SDPRP. Final absorption of MDG indicators 5.5 and 5.6 took place in the GTP.

3.3 Possible explanations for different levels of MDG absorption into Ethiopia's PRSPs

The above analysis provides an in-depth view into how MDG 2 and 5 were included into Ethiopia's PRSPs. For both MDGs there was already one indicator, which was explicitly included in the preliminary version of Ethiopia's PRSP in 2000: primary education enrollment rate and maternal mortality rate. Absorption of MDG 2 and 5 into Ethiopia's PRSPs proceeded similarly, however, somewhat different. In the case of MDG 2, the majority of indicators were successfully included, with specific targets and detailed measures, in the second generation of PRSPs, the PASDEP. For MDG 5, most indicators were already added in the first generation of PRSP, the SDPRP.

Comparing the current status of MDGs' achievement in Ethiopia with their absorption in the PRSP shows that the earlier an MDG indicator was incorporated into the PRSP, the higher is the probability for achievement. Moreover, the more priority was given to a certain indicator in the PRSP by the government, the better the results of the MDGs. Lastly, the deeper and better incorporated the respective indicator was into the PRSP, national policies and programs, the more likely the achievement of the MDG. The achievements in GERP and MMR are leading examples for this: targets for both indicators are already reached or will be reached by 2015. In turn, the achievement of targets of other late incorporated indicators of less priority, such as literacy rate is still questionable. This proves that the content of and priority setting within the PRSPs play indeed a crucial role in explaining the (non-) achievement of the MDGs.

The reason for the different absorption processes of MDG 2 and MDG 5 lies to some extent with the national government and how important they viewed the issue at stake. At the same time, development partners such as the UN country team are accountable for the (un-) successful incorporation of MDG targets into PRSPs as they are highly influencing the actual PRSPs (IMF, 2013a; 2013b). In general, how well or bad MDGs have been absorbed into the PRSPs can be explained considering the actual purpose of the PRSPs themselves: PRSPs generally pursue a focus on economic growth and poverty reduction. Although PRSPs are supposed to adhere to the principle 'multi-dimensional', this aspect has often been neglected as attention has been put first and foremost on income poverty, thus leading to a belated inclusion of crosscutting MDG issues.

4 Outlook of PRSPs in terms of the post-2015 Agenda

With the definition of SDGs, ongoing discussions on the post-2015 agenda allow to forecast that the focus of upcoming MDGs will most probably move away from a single-centered poverty-reduction-approach to one which emphasizes inequality, the provision of global public goods and sustainability (Kaul, 2013; Sachs, 2012). Hence, PRSPs, with their initial purpose of outlining poverty reduction and growth strategies, need to be revised to become central, powerful tools in achieving the post-2015 agenda. Most importantly is to not only adhere but also to deeply incorporate and expand on the principles 'comprehensive', 'country ownership' and 'partnership-oriented' as these are at the root of the post-2015 agenda.

5 Bibliography

Adejumobi, S. 2006. Governance and Poverty Reduction in Africa: A Critique of the Poverty Reduction Strategy Papers (PRSPs). In: University of Texas, *Inter-Regional Conference on Social Policy and Welfare Regimes in Comparative Perspectives*. Austin, April, 20-22.

Afrodad. 2006. Linking PRSPs and the Millennium Development Goals: the Case of Ethiopia. Viewed on 10th June 2013. Accessed at <http://www.afrodad.org/Publications/PRSP-Poverty%20Reduction%20Strategy%20Papers/Linkinf%20PRSPs%20and%20MDGs/ethiopia%20prsps%20mdgs.pdf>.

Bucki, P, Callaghan, S., Khalid, U., Morony, C., Phillips, J., Tsedendamba, A. & Varela, A. 2013. Absorption of the Millenium Development Goals into Poverty Reduction Strategy Papers. *The Heinz Journal*, 10 (2): 29-56.

CIA. 2013. *Ethiopia*. Viewed on 12th June 2013. Accessed at <https://www.cia.gov/library/publications/the-world-factbook/geos/et.html>.

Eggen, A. & Bezemer, D. 2008. The Role of Poverty Reduction Strategies in Achieving the Millennium Development Goals. University of Groningen: Research Institute SOM.

Fraser, A. 2005. PRSPs: Now who calls the shots? *Review of African Political Economy,* 32 (104/105): 317-340.

Hulme, D. & Fukudu-Parr, S. 2009. International Norm Dynamics and 'the End of Poverty': Understanding the Millennium Development Goals (MDGs). BWPI Working Paper, 96. Manchester: Brooks World Poverty Institute.

IMF. 2013a. *Factsheet: Poverty Reduction Strategy Papers*. Viewed on 10th June 2013. Accessed at < http://www.imf.org/external/np/exr/facts/prsp.htm>.

IMF. 2013b. *Poverty Reduction Strategy Papers (PRSP) (All Documents)*. Viewed on 10th June 2013. Accessed at <http://www.imf.org/external/np/prsp/prsp.aspx>.

Kalinda, T. 2008. Growth and Poverty Focus of the PRSPs in HIPC Countries: the Case of Tanzania, Uganda and Zambia. In: Annual Bank Conference on Development Economics. Cape Town, June, 9-11.

Kaul, I. 2013. Global Public Goods: A Concept for Framing the Post-2015 Agenda? Discussion Paper 2/2013. Bonn: German Development Institute.

MDG Track. 2010. *MDGs: Where do we stand in Ethiopia?* Viewed on 12th June 2013. Accessed at <http://www.mdgtrack.org/index.php?tab=c&c=ETH>.

Ministry of Finance and Economic Development (MoFED). 2011a. Ethiopia: Poverty Reduction Strategy Paper: Growth and Transformation Plan 2010/11–2014/15 – Volume I. Viewed on 12th June 2013. Accessed at <http://www.imf.org/external/pubs/ft/scr/2011/cr11305.pdf>.

Ministry of Finance and Economic Development (MoFED). 2011b. Ethiopia: Poverty Reduction Strategy Paper: Growth and Transformation Plan 2010/11–2014/15 – Volume II. Viewed on 12th June 2013. Accessed at <http://www.imf.org/external/pubs/ft/scr/2011/cr11304.pdf>.

Ministry of Finance and Economic Development (MoFED). 2010. Ethiopia: 2010 MDG Report. Trends and Prospects for Meeting MDGs by 2015. Viewed on 11th June 2013. Accessed at <http://www.undp.org/content/dam/undp/library/MDG/english/MDG%20Country%20Reports/Ethiopia/ethiopia_september2010.pdf>.

Ministry of Finance and Economic Development (MoFED). 2006. Ethiopia: Building on Progress. A Plan for Accelerated and Sustained Development to End Poverty (PASDEP). Viewed on 12th June 2013. Accessed at < http://www.afdb.org/fileadmin/uploads/afdb/Documents/Policy-Documents/Plan_for_Accelerated_and_Sustained_(PASDEP)_final_July_2007_Volume_I_3.pdf>.

Ministry of Finance and Economic Development (MoFED). 2002. Ethiopia: Sustainable Development and Poverty Reduction Program. Viewed on 12th June 2013. Accessed at <http://www.imf.org/External/NP/prsp/2002/eth/01/073102.pdf>.

Ministry of Finance and Economic Development (MoFED). 2000. Ethiopia: Interim Poverty Reduction Strategy Paper 2000/01- 2002/03. Viewed on 12th June 2013. Accessed at <http://www.imf.org/external/NP/prsp/2000/eth/01/113000.pdf>.

Ministry of Foreign Affairs (Ethiopia). 2013. *Pro-poor development: Ethiopia and partners' co-operation.* Viewed on 13th June 2013. Accessed at <http://www.mfa.gov.et/pressMore.php?pg=45>.

Oxfam. 2004. From 'Donorship' to Ownership? Moving Towards PRSP Round Two. Briefing Paper, Washington: Oxfam International.

Picard, L. A., Buss, T. F. & Belasco, C. 2010. The Effectiveness of Aid and the Millennium Development Goals in Advancing Human Development, 1990 to 2010. New York: United Nations Development Programme, Human Development Report.

Provost, C. 2013. 2013 Millennium Development Goal Progress Index – Get the Data. *The Guardian.* [online]. May, 29. Viewed on 12th June 2013. Accessed at <http://www.guardian.co.uk/global-development/poverty-matters/2013/may/29/millennium-development-goal-progress-data>.

Sachs, J. D. 2012. From Millennium Development Goals to Sustainable Development Goals. *The Lancet,* 379: 2206-2011.

UNDP. 2013. MDG Report 2013: Assessing Progress in Africa toward the Millennium Development Goals. Viewed on 11th June 2013. Accessed at <http://www.undp.org/content/dam/undp/library/MDG/english/MDG%20Regional%20Reports/Africa/MDG%20report%202013%20summary_EN.pdf>.

United Nations. 2008. Official List of MDG Indicators. Viewed on 12th June 2013. Accessed at <http://mdgs.un.org/unsd/mdg/Host.aspx?Content=Indicators/OfficialList.htm>.

World Bank. 2012. Board Presentations of JSAN on Country-owned PRSPs. Viewed on 11th June 2013. Accessed at <http://siteresources.worldbank.org/INTPRS1/Resources/boardlist.pdf>.

World Bank. 2013a. Poverty & Equity: Ethiopia. Viewed on 12th June 2013. Accessed at < http://povertydata.worldbank.org/poverty/country/ETH>.

World Bank. 2013b. Ethiopia Overview. Viewed on 12th June 2013. Accessed at <http://www.worldbank.org/en/country/ethiopia/overview>.